# Contents

# All Kinds of Food

Are you ready to travel around the world and find out about the food eaten by children just like you? You'll learn what people eat to start the day and to celebrate a special day. There are sweet treats and delicious drinks to discover, too.

There are different festival foods around the world. What foods can you see at this American Thanksgiving meal? Find out on page 13.

Different fruit and vegetables grow in each country. Learn the name of this bright pink Mexican fruit on page 20.

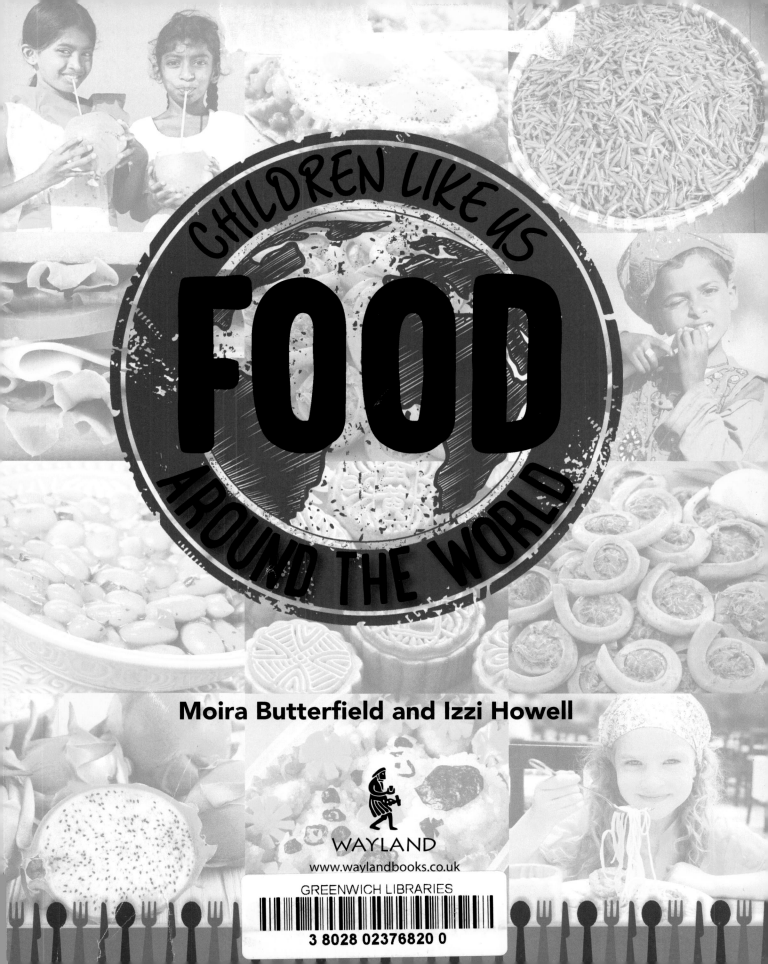

# CHILDREN LIKE US
# FOOD
## AROUND THE WORLD

## Moira Butterfield and Izzi Howell

**WAYLAND**
www.waylandbooks.co.uk

Published in paperback in 2017
by Wayland

© Hodder and Stoughton, 2017

All rights reserved.

ISBN: 978 0 7502 9713 4

10 9 8 7 6 5 4 3

An Hachette UK Company
www.hachette.co.uk
www.hachettechildrens.co.uk

Printed in China

Produced for Wayland by:
White-Thomson Publishing Ltd
www.wtpub.co.uk

Editor: Izzi Howell
Designer: Clare Nicholas
Picture researcher: Izzi Howell
Proofreaders: Izzi Howell/Stephen White-Thomson
Wayland editor: Annabel Stones

Picture credits:
The author and publisher would like to thank the following for allowing their pictures to be reproduced in this publication: cover (l-r, t-b) Peathegee Inc/Blend Images/Corbis, Lauri Patterson/iStock, Gil Giuglio/Hemis/Corbis, mipstudio/Shutterstock, tbradford/iStock, vertmedia/iStock, Sarah Bossert/iStock, enviromantic/iStock, Nataliya Arzamasova/Shutterstock, Philippe Lissac/Godong/Corbis; back cover (t/b) tbradford/iStock, (l) Isantilli/Shutterstock, (r) neelsky/Shutterstock; title page (l-r, t-b) Bartosz Hadyniak/iStock, Lauri Patterson/iStock, tbradford/iStock, mipstudio/Shutterstock, neelsky/Shutterstock, vertmedia/iStock, fotohunter/Shutterstock, Sarah Bossert/iStock, enviromantic/iStock, Nataliya Arzamasova/Shutterstock, Tatyana Gladskikh/Dreamstime; p.3 (t-b) mkistryn/iStock, Perfect Lazybones/Shutterstock, Nataliya Arzamasova/Shutterstock, Sarah Bossert/iStock; pp.4-5 (c) ekler/Shutterstock, p.4 (t) bhofack2/iStock, (b) enviromantic/iStock; p.5 (tl) bonchan/iStock, (tr) szefei/Shutterstock, (b) idome/Shutterstock; p.6 (t) xuanhuongho/Shutterstock, (b) bonchan/iStock; p.7 (l) Amanda Koster/Corbis, (r) Lauri Patterson/iStock; p.8 (t) szefei/Shutterstock, (bl) Nataliya Arzamasova/Shutterstock, (br) HLPhoto/Shutterstock; p.9 Ron Nickel/Design Pics/Corbis; p.10 (tl) Africa Studio/Shutterstock, (tr) Tatyana Gladskikh/Dreamstime, (b) Staffan Widstrand/Corbis; p.11 (l) Gil Giuglio/Hemis/Corbis, (r) picturepartners/Shutterstock; p.12 (t) Hasse Bengtsson/Johnér Images/Corbis, (b) Krzysztof Slusarczyk/Shutterstock, p.13 (t) Isantilli/Shutterstock, (b) bhofack2/iStock; p.14 (t) Oleg Baliuk/Shutterstock, (b) Li Luan Han /Redlink/Redlink/Corbis; p.15 IndiaImages/iStock; p.16 (tl) Chen Li/Xinhua Press/Corbis, (tr) fotohunter/Shutterstock, (b) pamspix/iStock; p.17 neelsky/Shutterstock; p.18 (t) eurobanks/iStock, (b) Bartosz Hadyniak/iStock; p.19 (t) Bartosz Hadyniak/iStock, (b) Stringer/India/Reuters/Corbis; p.20 (t) Tomophafan/Shutterstock, (bl) enviromantic/iStock, (br) mkistryn/iStock; p.21 javarman/Shutterstock; p.22 Yadid Levy/Robert Harding World Imagery/Corbis; p.23 (tr) JMWScout/iStock, (c) Sarah Bossert/iStock, (bl) xuanhuongho/iStock; p.24 (tl) Bartosz Hadyniak/iStock, (cr) Sarah Bossert/iStock, (br) Elena Mirage/Shutterstock; p.25 Owen Franken/Corbis; p.26 (t) astudio/Shutterstock, (b) Orietta Gaspari/Shutterstock; p.27 (t) Peathegee Inc/Blend Images/Corbis, (b) Perfect Lazybones/Shutterstock; pp.28-29 Remi Benali/Corbis; p.29 (l) idome/Shutterstock, (r) Perfect Lazybones/Shutterstock; p.30 (l-r, t-b) neelsky/Shutterstock, enviromantic/iStock, vertmedia/iStock, Nataliya Arzamasova/Shutterstock, bonchan/iStock, eurobanks/iStock, idome/Shutterstock, Isantilli/Shutterstock, mipstudio/Shutterstock, mkistryn/iStock, Africa Studio/Shutterstock, fotohunter/Shutterstock, Tatyana Gladskikh/Dreamstime, HLPhoto/Shutterstock; p.31 (l) javarman/Shutterstock, (r) IndiaImages/iStock.

Design elements used throughout: Oksancia/Shutterstock, lilac/Shutterstock, Dacian G/Shutterstock, rassco/Shutterstock, Aliaksei_7799/Shutterstock, Jane Rix/Shutterstock, id-work/iStock, pandora64/Shutterstock, AKIllustration/Shutterstock, PinkPueblo/Shutterstock, ksana-gribakina/Shutterstock, Turkan Akyol/Shutterstock, kasahasa/Shutterstock, oxygendesign021/Shutterstock, akiradesigns/Shutterstock, tsirik/Shutterstock, Anton Lunkov/Shutterstock, rustamank/Shutterstock, LSF421/Shutterstock, Macrovector/Shutterstock.

Some people start the day with something sweet. Find out about Spanish churros on page 6.

People eat all kinds of lunchtime foods. Discover the story behind this Indian dish on page 8.

Street markets sell many types of snacks. Can you imagine what Cambodian fried tarantulas taste like? Find out the answer on page 29.

Take a journey around the world to discover some fantastic food eaten by children just like you!

# What's for Breakfast?

This lady is serving up a Vietnamese bowl of breakfast, a noodle soup called pho. It's a spicy broth made with chicken or beef and rice noodles. If you visited a Vietnamese town, you would find pho cafés and street stalls busy serving steaming bowls of pho for breakfast.

It takes many hours to boil up a good pho broth and get it tasting just right.

If you like the idea of chocolate sauce for breakfast, make sure you try churros from Spain. You can buy these sugary fried dough sticks in local morning markets, freshly cooked and still warm, along with a pot of chocolate sauce for dipping.

Churros sometimes get dipped in thick hot chocolate or milky coffee.

A corn tortilla is topped with tomato sauce, beans, rice and eggs for the popular Mexican breakfast dish of huevos rancheros.

This Guatemalan girl is holding a bowl of ground corn paste, which will be flattened and cooked to make tortillas. This mixture is called masa.

In Central America, corn tortillas are often eaten at breakfast time. Tortillas can be used in different ways – wrapped around meat or eggs, cut into strips and fried, or baked with tomato sauce and cheese.

# What's for Lunch?

These little piles of spicy Indian food are called chaat, snack-sized portions put together to make a tasty lunch. The legend goes that when an Indian emperor called Sha Jahan fell ill, his doctor invented chaat to help cure him. In India, spices are regarded as healthy medicine.

This chaat lunch is being served on a banana leaf.

Here is a kawaii bento box. The rice and vegetables have been made into a picture of two pandas.

In Japan, children often take bento boxes to school for their packed lunches. Bento boxes contain small portions of different foods, such as cooked and pickled vegetables and rice. Making a kawaii bento box is a popular hobby in Japan. Kawaii bento boxes contain food made into pictures. The word 'kawaii' means 'cute' in Japanese.

A normal bento box might contain sushi – rolls of rice and vegetables, and sashimi – raw fish.

This girl from Mozambique in Africa is having a typical African lunch of rice and beans, made into a spicy stew. The beans might be kidney beans, black beans or peas, flavoured with salt, onions, chilli and red pepper.

Different versions of rice and beans are served all over Africa.

# What's for Dinner?

Do you sometimes have pasta for dinner? According to a survey by the charity Oxfam, pasta is now the most popular food in the world! Pasta was first made in Italy almost 1,000 years ago. At that time, they used lettuce juice to give the pasta a green colour.

There are around 500 different kinds of pasta, each with its own Italian name. Look for some different types in the shops, then see if you can find out what their names mean.

This girl is having 'little strings' for dinner. That's the meaning of the Italian word 'spaghetti'.

In the icy far north of Canada, there aren't many shops or restaurants. People find it easier and cheaper to hunt for their dinner, killing and cooking the wild food they find. This Nunavut boy is catching arctic charr, a type of fish, from the Arctic Ocean through a hole in the ice.

In the far north, the Arctic Ocean is covered with ice for most of the year. Fishing through a hole is the only way for the Nunavut to catch fish.

This Tunisian boy is buying spices in a souk, a traditional North African outdoor market. These spices will be used to flavour his dinner of kosksi – couscous served with spicy meat and vegetables. Most people in Tunisia are Muslims, so they do not eat pork. Dishes are made with lamb, beef, chicken and vegetables.

In the Tunisian dish of kosksi, meat and vegetables are served on top of couscous.

Tunisian food is often flavoured with harissa - a spicy paste made of roasted peppers and dried spices.

# Festival Food

Food is important at all kinds of festivals. In Sweden, they celebrate St. Lucia's Day on 13 December by eating saffron-flavoured buns, called lussekat. On the morning of St. Lucia's Day, the oldest girl in a family gives her parents a plate of lussekat buns for breakfast.

This Swedish girl is helping to bake lussekat buns for St Lucia's Day.

In Swedish, lussekat means 'Lucia's cats'. The buns were given this name because some people think they look like cats.

A special meal of lentils and spicy pork sausages is served at New Year's Eve celebrations in Italy. The lentils symbolise good fortune, and the pork represents the richness of life. Everybody eats some of the dish to make sure they have good luck in the coming year!

These Italian New Year lentils and sausage slices are coin-shaped, representing the money everybody hopes to get in the months to come.

The Thanksgiving celebration in the USA is a great example of food with a special story. In 1620, the Wampanoag Native American people helped the first European settlers survive by offering them local food, including turkeys, cranberries and pumpkin. Now these foods appear on the Thanksgiving Day table.

On Thanksgiving Day in the USA, traditional foods such as turkey and cranberries are eaten to celebrate American history.

# Wedding Food

The tradition of eating a wedding cake dates all the way back to Ancient Roman times, around 2,000 years ago. At the end of an Ancient Roman wedding ceremony, the groom broke a small cake made of wheat over the bride's head, and the guests ate the crumbs to share the couple's good fortune.

At modern weddings, the bride and groom cut the wedding cake and share it with their guests.

This Chinese bride is giving out sweets to her wedding guests. Chinese wedding sweets are often made from peanuts and sugar, coated with crunchy sesame seeds. They are a symbol of sweetness and harmony – perfect for a wedding!

These Chinese wedding guests are being treated to a feast of many different dishes.

These Indian women are taking part in a four-day wedding feast. There will be a lot more eating to do before the end of the wedding!

All around the world, there is usually a special meal laid on for the guests at a wedding. In India, it's more than just one dinner. It's a four-day feast! At the end of the festivities, any leftover food gets shared around the local village, so everybody gets a tasty wedding treat.

# Sweet Treats

During the Chinese Moon Festival, it's traditional to eat little mooncakes filled with bean paste and egg yolks, like the ones being made here. The cakes have Chinese characters on top. Legend has it that they were once used to pass secret messages between Chinese rebels fighting invaders.

Modern mooncakes have messages, such as 'long life', written on them in Chinese characters.

In the past, mooncakes were eaten to honour a Chinese moon goddess.

Anzac biscuits are made with oats, coconut and syrup. Try baking some yourself. They're delicious!

On 25 April, sweet buttery Anzac biscuits are eaten in Australia and New Zealand. They are made to commemorate Anzac Day, when people remember the soldiers who fought in World Wars I and II. Anzac biscuits were first made in Australia and New Zealand during the war, to send to soldiers fighting overseas.

This Indian boy is enjoying a snack of raw sugarcane. You can't eat the hard outer part of the cane, but when you chew the soft inner core, sugary juice comes out. Sugarcane is too sweet to be eaten every day, but it's a fun treat at festivals or fairs.

This stick of raw sugarcane will keep this Indian boy busy for a long time.

# Delicious Drinks

Bubble tea tastes like a sweet milky smoothie, with added chewy bits.

Have you tried bubble tea yet? It was invented in Taiwan in the 1980s and now the craze has spread to other countries. You can buy all sorts of flavoured bubble teas and drink it hot or cold, with chewy tapioca or jelly balls floating at the bottom.

This young Tibetan monk is making a big vat of butter tea.

If you visited somebody living in Tibet, you would be offered butter tea, made from tea leaves mixed with yak butter, salt and water. It's considered rude to ever leave a guest's cup empty, so your host will keep filling your cup until you leave!

Moroccan mint tea is poured from a height to give it a better flavour.

These Sri Lankan girls are enjoying a refreshing drink of coconut water, drunk straight from the coconut. You only need to drill or cut a hole into a coconut and add a straw for an instant drink!

You can only drink coconut water from young coconuts that haven't developed a hard outer shell.

# Fantastic Fruit

This is the world's smelliest fruit! It's called a durian, and it's grown in Malaysia. It is said to smell like rotting onions mixed with sweaty socks, but its soft flesh tastes like ripe banana. Durians are so smelly that they are banned on trains in Singapore and in some airports and hotels.

The durian fruit is soft inside, and unbelievably stinky!

This yellow fruit is a Buddha's Hand from India. It tastes like a lemon and it's sometimes taken to Buddhist temples as a religious offering. The pretty pink fruit is a pitahaya, or dragon fruit, from Mexico and Central America. It tastes similar to watermelon.

Pitahayas grow on spiky cactus plants.

This lady is selling fruit in a market in the city of Cartagena, Colombia. Her basket of tropical fruits includes pineapple and melon, which people in Europe had never seen or tasted until Europeans arrived in the Americas in 1492.

Tropical fruits were once only available to people who lived in tropical regions. Now they are sent around the world to be enjoyed in every country.

As well as being eaten, the Buddha's Hand fruit is sometimes kept in a room as a lemon-scented air freshener.

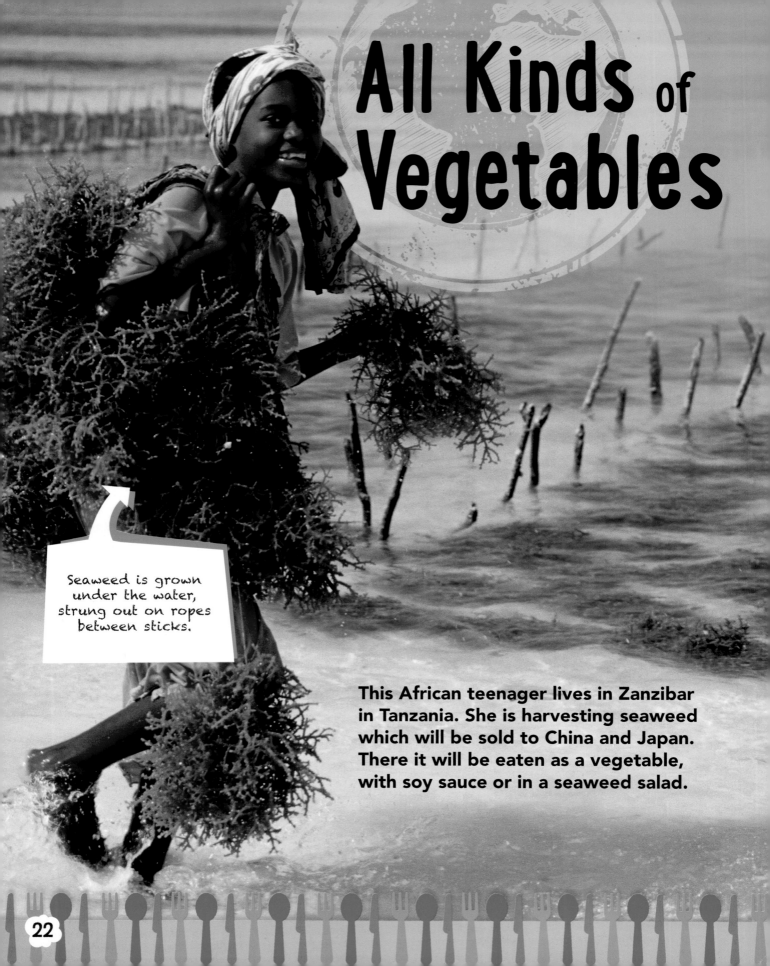

# All Kinds of Vegetables

Seaweed is grown under the water, strung out on ropes between sticks.

This African teenager lives in Zanzibar in Tanzania. She is harvesting seaweed which will be sold to China and Japan. There it will be eaten as a vegetable, with soy sauce or in a seaweed salad.

This person is cutting up nopales, the pads of a prickly pear cactus with the spikes removed. Nopales are popular in Mexico. They taste a little like green beans. The round curly vegetables are the edible tips of fern plants, called fiddleheads. They are eaten in New England, USA.

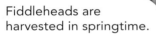

Fiddleheads are harvested in springtime.

Nopales are fried or used in salads.

In this Vietnamese market, you can buy different kinds of root vegetables (edible plant roots that grow underground), such as taro, manioc and sweet potatoes. In tropical parts of the world, people cook these root vegetables like potatoes or grind them up to make flour.

The large, brown root vegetables that this Vietnamese man is selling are called manioc. Manioc is used to make tapioca, which is what the bubbles in bubble tea are made from (see page 18).

# Scrummy Bread

Bread is eaten all around the world. There are lots of different kinds of bread that look and taste different from each other. Across Asia and Africa, flatbread is really popular. People bake flatbreads on open fires and sell them on roadside stalls.

In Ethiopia, a flatbread called injera is used instead of a plate! People use small pieces of the injera to scoop up the food which is served on top of it.

Flatbreads are round and flat, like thick pancakes.

Sometimes bread has its own special story. These big round loaves, called tokoch, are being sold at a market in Kyrgyzstan in Asia. It is said that if you want good luck, you should bake seven tokoch loaves and give them to seven different people.

In Kyrgyzstan, you might be offered a piece of tokoch with some homemade plum jam.

These Turkish simit loaves are being sold fresh from the oven.

This Turkish boy is selling delicious simit – a round loaf covered in crunchy sesame seeds. He might be calling out: 'Taze Simit!' (fresh simit) or perhaps 'Sicak simit!' (hot simit). Simit has been sold like this for many centuries in Turkey and Greece.

# Street Eating

Hot spicy sausages are traditional German street food.

Around Christmas time, German towns hold Christmas markets. Here, the street food includes hot sausages and potatoes, to keep you warm, and traditional spiced gingerbread biscuits to remind you that Christmas is here!

Sweets, nuts and gingerbread are usually on sale at German Christmas markets.

These children are enjoying snow cones from a food truck in Los Angeles, USA. Food trucks are vans fitted with kitchens so that food can be prepared on board. Food trucks park on streets or at events and sell all kinds of food; from sweets to pizza.

Snow cones are a popular treat in America. They are made by pouring flavoured syrup over crushed ice!

This woman is selling street food in a market in Cambodia, southeast Asia. Her basket is filled with num kom, steamed banana leaf packages filled with rice dough and sweet coconut. Like many street food sellers around the world, she probably makes the food herself every day, and sells it to make a living.

The word 'num' means cake in Khmer, the language of Cambodia.

# Now THAT'S Different!

This Sumatran boy is eating crunchy ants straight from the nest because they taste sweet, like honey. Insects are cooked and eaten in many African and Asian countries. They are full of protein, which is important in a balanced diet.

Ants are sometimes fried or toasted, and even made into cakes.

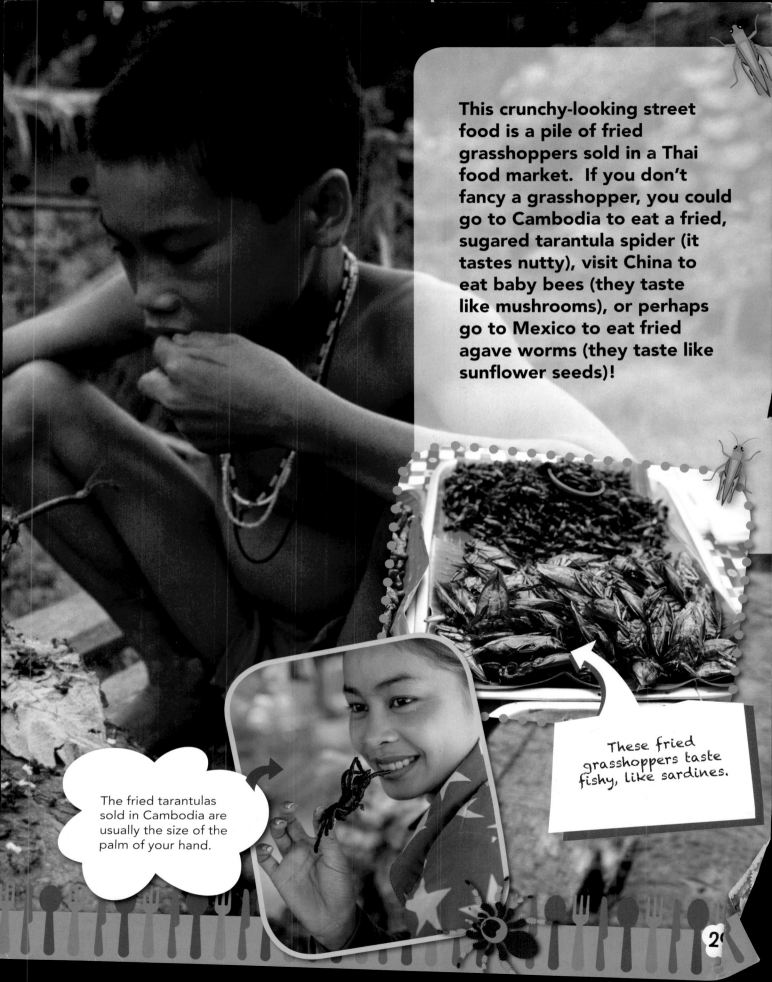

This crunchy-looking street food is a pile of fried grasshoppers sold in a Thai food market. If you don't fancy a grasshopper, you could go to Cambodia to eat a fried, sugared tarantula spider (it tastes nutty), visit China to eat baby bees (they taste like mushrooms), or perhaps go to Mexico to eat fried agave worms (they taste like sunflower seeds)!

These fried grasshoppers taste fishy, like sardines.

The fried tarantulas sold in Cambodia are usually the size of the palm of your hand.

# Art Station

Here are some ideas to help you get creative and become an amazing chef!

- What is your favourite breakfast dish? Draw a picture of it and label the ingredients.

- Invent a new dish using fruit. Draw a picture of it, give it a name and label the ingredients.

- Design a stall to sell street food. Work out what kind of food you're going to sell and give your stall a name.

- Design a cake for a party. It could be a wedding cake, a birthday cake or a celebration cake for some other kind of special occasion.

# Glossary

**bento box** a Japanese lunch box

**broth** another word for soup

**dough** flour mixed with water

**edible** something you can eat

**festival** a day or a period of a few days when everyone celebrates something

**flatbread** bread that does not have yeast in it to make it rise

**ingredients** types of food put together to make a recipe

**noodles** long thin strips made from different types of flour mixed with water

**pasta** strips or little shapes made from wheat flour mixed with water

**protein** a part of food that helps your body to grows strong and stay healthy

**root vegetable** the edible root of a plant

**spice** flavouring made from parts of a dried plant, such as seeds, roots or bark

**symbol** something that represents an idea

**tradition** something that has been going on for a long time

**tropical** hot weather found in parts of the world around the Equator, an imaginary line around the middle of the Earth

# Further Information

## Websites

**A slide show of families around the world and what they eat.**
http://time.com/8515/hungry-planet-what-the-world-eats/

**Food information about different countries around the globe.**
www.foodbycountry.com

**Street foods around the world.**
http://travel.nationalgeographic.com/travel/countries/street-food-photos/

## Further Reading

*Food and Cooking in India*
Rosemary Hankin (Wayland, 2014)

*My Holiday in Italy*
Jane Bingham (Wayland, 2014)

*Your Local Area*
Ruth Thomson (Wayland, 2013)

# Index